The Sorrows
of Work

The Sorrows
of Work

The School of Life

Published in 2017 by The School of Life
70 Marchmont Street, London WC1N 1AB
Copyright © The School of Life 2017
Designed and typeset by Marcia Mihotich
Printed in Latvia by Livonia Print

A proportion of this book has appeared online at
thebookoflife.org

Every effort has been made to contact the copyright holders of
the material reproduced in this book. If any have been
inadvertently overlooked, the publisher will be pleased to make
restitution at the earliest opportunity.

The School of Life offers programmes, publications and
services to assist modern individuals in their quest to live more
engaged and meaningful lives. We've also developed a collection
of content-rich, design-led retail products to promote useful
insights and ideas from culture.

www.theschooloflife.com

ISBN 978-0-9957535-1-8

Contents

I
Introduction

There is no more common emotion to feel around work than that we have failed. We have failed because we have made less money than we had hoped; because we have been sidelined in our organisation; because many of our acquaintances have triumphed; because our schemes have remained on the drawing board; because we have been constantly anxious and, for long stretches, tired and bored.

We tend to meet our sorrows personally. We believe that our failures are tightly bound up with our own character and choices. But the suggestion here is that the single greatest cause of our professional failure lies in an area that self-aware, moderate and modest people are instinctively loath to blame: the system we live within. Whatever our natural hesitancy, it seems we deserve to recast at least some of the explanations for our woes away from intimate experience and towards large-scale historical and economic forces. Although on a daily basis we are enmeshed in problems (inadequacies, desires and panics) that feel as if they must be our responsibility alone, the real causes may lie far beyond ourselves, in the greater, grander currents of history: in the way our industries are structured, our values are determined, and our assumptions generated. For a long time now, capitalism has been a confirmedly tricky system in which to retain equilibrium, make peace with ourselves, find fulfilment in our work – and cope. It's not quite our fault if, rather too often, we feel like losers.

This isn't to make a particular dig at capitalism, or to suggest that there may be easier alternatives at hand. Every economy that has ever existed has been bound up with multiple sorrows. Organising an equitable system of incentives, goads and rewards is as yet beyond us. We should be allowed to level criticisms, not in the name of arguing for an alternative utopia, but in order to depersonalise our sense of failure.

Work disappoints us, not by coincidence but by necessity, for at least eight central reasons:

1. The demand for specialisation limits our potential.

2. The concentration of capital squeezes out personal initiative.

3. The extent of consumer choice forces us to commercialise our work beyond what feels tolerable.

4. The scale of industry robs us of a sense of meaning.

5. Competition generates a state of perpetual anxiety.

6. The requirement for collaboration maddens us.

7. Our high aspirations embitter us.

8. The notion that the world is meritocratic imposes a crushing burden of responsibility on us for our defeats.

Understanding the sorrows of work will not magically remove them, but it at least spares us the burden of feeling that we must be uniquely stupid and clumsy for suffering them.

II
Specialisation

One of the greatest sorrows of work stems from a sense that only a small portion of our talents has been taken up and engaged by the job we have signed up to do every day. We are likely to be so much more than our labour allows us to be. The title on our business card is only one of thousands of titles we theoretically possess.

In his 'Song of Myself', published in 1855, the American poet Walt Whitman (1819–1892) gave our multiplicity memorable expression: 'I am large, I contain multitudes' – by which he meant that there are many interesting, attractive and viable versions of oneself, many good ways one could potentially live and work, and yet very few of these are ever properly played out in the course of the single life we have. No wonder that we are quietly and painfully conscious of our unfulfilled destinies, and at times recognise, with a legitimate sense of agony, that we could have been something and someone else.

The major economic reason why we cannot explore our potential as we might is that it is much more productive for us not to do so. In *The Wealth of Nations*, published in 1776, the Scottish economist and philosopher Adam Smith (1723–1790) first explained how what he termed the 'division of labour' was at the heart of the increased productivity of capitalism. Smith zeroed in on the dazzling efficiency that could be achieved in pin manufacturing, if everyone focused on one narrow task (and stopped, as it were, exploring their Whitman-esque 'multitudes'):

> One man draws out the wire, another straights it, a third cuts it, a fourth points it, a fifth grinds it at the top for receiving the head; to make the head requires two or three distinct operations; to put it on is a peculiar business, to whiten the pins is another; it is even a trade by itself to put them into the paper; and the important business of making a pin is, in this manner, divided into about eighteen distinct operations, all performed by distinct hands. I have seen a small manufactory where they could make upwards of forty-eight thousand pins in a day. But if they had all wrought separately and independently, and without any of them having been educated to this peculiar business, they could have made perhaps not one pin in a day.

> – Adam Smith, *The Wealth of Nations*, Book 1, Chapter 1, *Of the Division of Labour* (1776)

Adam Smith was astonishingly prescient. Doing one job, preferably for most of one's life, makes perfect economic sense. It is a tribute to the world that Smith foresaw – and

The title on our business card is only one of thousands of titles we theoretically possess.

helped to bring into being – that we have ended up doing such specific jobs, and carry titles like Senior Packaging & Branding Designer, Intake and Triage Clinician, Research Centre Manager, Risk and Internal Audit Controller, and Transport Policy Consultant. We have become tiny, relatively wealthy cogs in giant, efficient machines. And yet, in our quiet moments, we reverberate with private longings to give our multitudinous selves expression.

One of Adam Smith's most intelligent and penetrating readers was the German economist Karl Marx (1818–1883). Marx agreed entirely with Smith's analysis; specialisation had indeed transformed the world and possessed a revolutionary power to enrich individuals and nations. But where he differed from Smith was in his assessment of how desirable this development might be. We would certainly make ourselves wealthier by specialising, but – as Marx pointed out with passion – we would also dull our lives and cauterise our talents. In describing his utopian communist society, Marx placed enormous emphasis on the idea of everyone having many different jobs. There were to be no specialists here. In a pointed dig at Smith, Marx wrote:

In communist society . . . nobody has one exclusive sphere of activity but each can become accomplished in any branch he wishes . . . thus it is possible for me to do one thing today and another tomorrow, to hunt in the morning, to fish in the afternoon, rear cattle in the evening, criticize after dinner . . . without ever becoming a hunter, fisherman, shepherd or critic.

– Karl Marx, *The German Ideology* (1846)

One reason why the job we do (and the jobs we don't get to do) matters so much is that our occupations decisively shape who we are. How our characters are marked by work is often hard for us to notice, as our outlooks just feel natural to us, but we can observe the identity-defining nature of work well enough in the presence of practitioners from different fields. The primary school teacher treats even the middle-aged a little as if they were in need of careful shepherding; the psychoanalyst has a studied way of listening and seeming not to judge while exuding a pensive, reflexive air; the politician lapses into speeches at intimate dinner parties.

Every occupation weakens or reinforces aspects of our nature. There are jobs that keep us constantly tethered to the immediate moment (A&E nurse, news editor); others that train our attention on the outlying fringes of the time horizon (futurist, urban planner, reforester). Certain jobs daily sharpen our suspicions of our fellow humans, suggesting that the real agenda must always be far from what is being said overtly (journalist, antique dealer); other sorts intersect with people at candid, intimate moments of their lives (anaesthetist, hairdresser, funeral director). In some jobs, it is clear what you have to do to move forward and how promotion occurs (civil servant, lawyer, surgeon), a dynamic that lends calm and steadiness to the soul, and diminishes tendencies to plot and manoeuvre. In other jobs (television producer, politician), the rules are muddied and seem bound up with accidents of friendship and fortuitous alliances, inspiring tendencies to anxiety, distrust and shiftiness.

The psychology inculcated by work doesn't neatly stay at work; it colours the whole of who we end up being. We start to behave across our whole lives like the people work has required us to be. This tends to narrow character. When certain ways of thinking become called for daily, others start to feel peculiar or threatening. By giving a large part of one's life over to a specific occupation, one necessarily has to perform an injustice to other areas of latent potential. Whatever enlargements it offers our personalities, work also possesses a powerful capacity to trammel our spirits.

We can offer ourselves the poignant autobiographical question of what sort of people we might have been had we had the opportunity to do something else. There will be parts of us we have had to kill (perhaps rather brutally) or that lie in shadow, twitching occasionally on Sunday afternoons. Contained within other career paths are other plausible versions of ourselves – which, when we dare to contemplate them, reveal important, but undeveloped or sacrificed, elements of our characters.

We are meant to be monogamous about our work, and yet truly have talents for many more jobs than we will ever have the opportunity to explore. We can understand the origins of our restlessness when we look back at our childhoods. As children, in a single Saturday morning, we might put on an extra jumper and imagine being an Arctic explorer, then have brief stints as an architect making a Lego house, a rock star making up an anthem about cornflakes and an inventor working out how to speed up colouring in by gluing four felt-tip pens together. We'd put in a few minutes as a member of an emergency rescue

Compared
to the play
of childhood,
we are leading
fatally
restricted
lives.

team, then we'd try out being a pilot, brilliantly landing a cargo plane on the rug in the corridor. We would perform a life-saving operation on a knitted rabbit, and then we'd find employment as a sous-chef helping make a ham and cheese sandwich for lunch. Each one of these 'games' might have been the beginning of a career. And yet we have to settle on only a single option, done repeatedly over the next 50 years.

Compared to the play of childhood, we are leading fatally restricted lives. There is no easy cure. As Adam Smith argued, the causes don't lie in some personal error; it is a limitation forced upon us by the greater logic of a productive, competitive market economy. However, we can allow ourselves to mourn that there will always be large aspects of our character that won't be satisfied. We are not being silly or ungrateful; we are simply registering the clash between the demands of the employment market and the free, wide-ranging potential of every human life. There is a touch of sadness to this insight. But it is also a reminder that this lack of fulfilment will accompany us in whatever job we choose: we shouldn't attempt to overcome it by switching jobs. No one job can ever be enough.

There is a parallel here between our experience around work and what happens in relationships. There is no doubt that we could (without any blame attaching to a current partner) have great relationships with dozens, maybe hundreds, of different people. They would bring to the fore different sides of our personality, please us (and upset us) in different ways, and introduce us to new excitements. Yet, as with work, specialisation brings advantages: it means we can focus, bring up children in stable environments, and learn the disciplines of compromise. In love and work, life requires us to be specialists even though we are by nature equally suited for wide-ranging exploration.

We carry about within us, in embryonic form, many alluring versions of ourselves that will never be given the proper chance to live. This is a sombre thought, but also a consoling one. Our suffering is painful, but has a curious dignity, because it does not uniquely affect us as individuals. It applies as much to the CEO as to the intern; to the artist as much as to the accountant. Everyone could have found so many versions of happiness that will elude them. In suffering in this way, we are participating in the common human lot. We may with a certain melancholic pride remove the job search engine from our bookmarks and cancel our subscription to a dating site in due recognition of the fact that, whatever we do, parts of our potential will have to go undeveloped and die without ever having had the chance to come to full maturity – for the sake of the benefits of focus and specialisation.

III
Standardisation

The sorrows of work are not limited to the likelihood that we will be somewhat unwillingly tied to a single field throughout our careers; even worse, our chosen field may turn out to be boring. We are liable to think that this fall into a tedious role must be our fault; a sign of our exceptional ineptitude. However, looked at dispassionately, boring jobs are an inherent and often unavoidable part of the modern economy.

When we speak of the opposite sort of job – an interesting job – we tend to refer to work that allows for a high degree of autonomy, personal initiative and (without anything artistic being meant by the word) creativity. In an interesting job, we won't simply be following orders; we will have latitude about what path we select to meet an objective or what we think the right solution to a problem might be. A good job, defined like this, is one that allows for a good measure of personalisation: we have an opportunity to directly imprint who we are in the work we produce. We end up seeing the best parts of our personalities in the objects or services we generate.

A lot of the writing about the nature of work produced in Europe and the United States in the 19th century can be read as an attempt to understand how personalisation disappeared from the labour market, even as wages rose. The English art critic and social reformer John Ruskin (1819–1900) proposed that the medieval building industry had been marked by a high degree of personalisation, evident in the way that craftsmen carved gargoyles (grotesque animal or human faces) in distinctive shapes high up on cathedral roofs. The stonemasons might have had to work to a fixed overall design, and their toil was not always easy, but the gargoyles symbolised a fundamental freedom to place their own stamp on their work. Ruskin added more ruefully that the new housing developments of the industrial age were allowing no such freedom or individualism to flourish in the workforce.

Ruskin's most devoted disciple, the poet and designer William Morris (1834–1896), extended the range of this idea of personalisation to a discussion of the making of furniture – his own area of expertise. Morris argued that the traditional way of making chairs and tables allowed artisans to see parts of themselves reflected in the character of the things they made. Every chair made by hand was as distinctive as its creator. In the pre-industrial age, thousands of people had been actively engaged in designing chairs, and every worker had been

Gargoyle, Sailsbury Cathedral

Art critic John Ruskin celebrated the latitude that medieval craftsmen had to create work imbued with their own unique style.

William Morris, Sussex chair, c. 1860

Morris believed that the process of making artefacts by hand imbued the piece with the unique character of the maker.

able to develop their own nuanced ideas about what a nice chair should be like.

However, an inevitable part of capitalism is a process of concentration and standardisation. There is a tendency for money, expertise, marketing clout and sophisticated distribution systems to be pooled together by a few big players, who outcompete and crush rivals and so achieve a daunting position in the marketplace. Barriers to entry rise exponentially. A well-financed operation can cut costs, assiduously research the preferences of consumers, marshal the best technology, and provide goods that can be of huge appeal to consumers at the best possible price. As a result, the artisanal mode of production cannot possibly compete – as Morris himself discovered when the traditional workshop that he established to make chairs for the Victorian middle classes was forced into receivership in the wake of a price war.

Today, there are, of course, still a few furniture designers around – some of them very well known – but this cannot disguise that what we call 'design' is quite a niche field employing a minuscule number of actors. The majority of those involved in the making and selling of furniture will have no opportunity to put their own character into the objects they are dealing with. They belong instead to a highly efficient army of labour that aims for rigorously anonymous execution.

Without intending to be mean-spirited or inherently hostile to the pleasures of work, capitalism has radically reduced the number of jobs that retain any component of personalisation.

For example, the Eames Aluminum Group chair was designed by American husband-and-wife team Charles (1907–1978) and Ray Eames (1912–1988) in 1958. It is a highly distinctive creation that reflects the ideals and outlook of the couple who designed it. If they had been artisans, operating their own small workshop, they might have sold a few dozen such chairs to their local customers in their lifetime. Instead, because they worked under capitalism for Herman Miller – a huge commercial office and home furniture manufacturing corporation – many hundreds of thousands of units have been, and continue to be, sold. A side effect of this triumph has been that the demand for well-designed, interesting chairs has been substantially cornered. Anyone wanting to make an office chair nowadays has to face the fact that it is already possible to buy a nice example, designed by

Charles and Ray Eames, Eames chair, 1958.

two geniuses and available for rapid delivery by a global company at a competitive price from a highly efficient network of local branches.

We are familiar with the idea that the wealth of the world is being ever more tightly concentrated in the hands of a relatively small number of people – the infamous '1%'. But capitalism doesn't only concentrate money. There's a more poignant, less familiar fact that only a small number of people – a sometimes overlapping, but often different 1% – have interesting, as in 'personalised', work.

It is telling that we are, at the same time, obsessed with the romance of individual genius. Our society has developed a near-fetishistic interest in the exploits of brilliant startups, colourful fashion gurus, and idiosyncratic film-makers and artists – characters who flamboyantly mould parts of the world in their own image and put their individual stamp on the things they do and make. We might like to think that we turn to them for inspiration, but it may be more the case that we use them to compensate ourselves for a painful gap in our own lives. The stories of successful personalisation have come to the fore just when the practical opportunities for personalised work have diminished. In a similar way, it was in the 19th century, during mass migration to cities, that novels about rural life achieved unprecedented popularity among newly urban audiences. We may, through our addiction to stories of lone creative geniuses, be trying to draw sustenance from qualities that are in woefully short supply in our own day-to-day working lives.

The prevalence of stories of individual creativity feed the illusion that personalised work is more normal than it really is. The many interviews and profiles mask the fact that, for almost all of us, it will prove nearly impossible to compete against the great forces of standardisation. For this reason, far more than because of anything we have done ourselves, many of us are likely to find a considerable portion of our work awkwardly tedious and dispiritingly free of any opportunities to carve our own gargoyles.

IV
Commercialisation

A complaint regularly aired around many careers is that, in order to succeed at them, there is no option but to 'sell out'. It appears that we will inevitably face a choice between authenticity and penury on the one hand, and idiocy and wealth on the other. We are familiar with this complaint in the arts, of course. But the same dilemma shows up when an interesting restaurant seems unable to make a profit; when a specialist bread company goes into receivership; when a garden supply firm focusing on rare native plants can't get a foothold in the market; when a sincere news site can't turn a profit, or when an ethically based investment firm is doomed to operate on a tiny scale in comparison with its less high-minded competitors.

Behind the complaint lies a very understandable but ambitious yearning: that our most passionately held beliefs and enthusiasms should, relatively painlessly, and by virtue of their merits, become high priorities for others. Our instincts lead us to suppose that what we are convinced of should prove equally compelling to strangers.

Young children are particularly prone to this assumption. On meeting a new adult, they may enthusiastically suggest that they join them in playing a favourite game, perhaps brew something on the miniature kitchen stove, or impersonate one of their dolls, which shows how hard it is for a child to grasp how alien his or her pleasures might be to another person. Children aren't silly; they are just highly attuned to their own natures and are convinced that others will share their tastes. In a naive but representative way, they illustrate an instinct that stays with us all of our lives: the supposition that others will and must be moved by what moves us; that their value systems are, or should be, like ours; and that what we love can automatically be what the world loves.

The reality is often humiliatingly and enragingly different. A novel that is filled with subtle character analyses and that takes inventive risks with plot structure might sell only modestly, while one that pits good against evil in a predictable way, relies on well-tried narrative tricks and arrives at an implausibly happy ending will dominate the bestseller lists. A high-street chain might do a fabulous trade in cut-price dark grey polyester-cotton socks, while a thoughtful, original brand involving striking colour combinations and materials ethically sourced from Peru will fail to find a market.

It is tempting to arrive at a despairing conclusion: that the economy is inherently devoted to delivering a personal affront to the better aspects of human nature. The truth is much less vindictive, but the tendency for the market to overlook or at least remain cool in relation to our more sincere and earnest efforts is nevertheless real – and founded on a raft of identifiable and stubborn forces in economic and psychological life.

One of the most basic of these forces is choice. It is in the nature of a growing, successful economy always to expand the range of choices offered to a consumer, and thereby, always to minimise the a priori claims of any one product or service. We can track the characteristic features of this development in relation to media. In 1952, a BBC radio broadcast of Beethoven's Fifth Symphony attracted an audience of five million listeners – approximately 16% of the UK's adult population. Today, such a broadcast would claim a fraction of these numbers. What explains the difference is not – as some cultural pessimists might claim – that the UK population has over a few generations become less sensitive to the emotive force of German Romantic music; the fundamental difference is that today's audience has many more options. In 1952, there were very few competing sources of entertainment. People listened en masse to the classical end of BBC radio because there was nothing much else to do. A producer who worked in the corporation had a great deal more authority than today's equivalent, not on the basis of superior genius, but because his listeners had few viable alternatives. This, rather nicely, gave certain high-brow things more opportunity to be attended to; but it also meant that many substandard services and products could enjoy a far larger role than their intrinsic merit warranted.

We know from the study of certain natural habitats that in situations of abundant choice (the warm seas around the Seychelles, for example), attention goes towards members of the species that appear colourful, variegated and theatrical. Much the same holds true for companies amid the din and buzz of the human marketplace. What is brusquely called 'selling out' typically refers to a series of moves no more and no less sinister than the elaborate signalling to which all living things must submit in their efforts to be noticed. Amid plenty, products and services must throw their qualities into dramatic relief, puff out their virtues, sound more confident than they perhaps are, and lodge themselves in the minds of their distracted audiences with unabashed insistence. It is understandable if those who are committed to higher values may balk at such demands, resentfully condemning the pitilessness of an unfeasibly vulgar system.

There is another reason why modern audiences are likely to sidestep opportunities for high-minded consumption: because they are exhausted. Modern work demands a punishing amount from its participants. We typically return from our jobs in a state of depletion: frazzled, tired, bored, enervated, sad. In such a state, the products and services for which we will be in the mood have to be of a very particular cast. We may be too brutalised to care much about the suffering of others, or to think empathetically of unfortunates in faraway tea plantations or cotton fields. We may have endured too much tedium to stay patient with arguments that are intelligently reticent and studiously subtle. We may be too anxious to have the strength to explore the more sincere sections of our own minds. We may hate ourselves a bit too much to want to eat and drink only what is good for us. Our lives may be too lacking in meaning to concentrate only on what is meaningful. To counterbalance what has happened at work, we may instinctively gravitate towards what is excessively sweet, salty, distracting, easy, colourful, explosive, sexual and sentimental.

This collectively creates a vicious circle. What we consume ends up determining what we produce – and, in turn, the quality of jobs that are on offer. So long as we only have the emotional resources to consume at the more narcotic and compromised end of the market, we will only generate employment that is itself challenged in meaning and compromised in dignity – which will further increase our demand for lower-order goods and services. We seem hampered by our existing conditions of employment from properly developing the sort of temperaments that could strengthen the sincerity and seriousness of our appetites and so expand the range of meaningful and non-depleting jobs we could have access to.

The price we pay for a marketplace that refuses to support high-minded efforts is not just practical and economic; it is also at some level emotional. One of our greatest cravings is to be recognised and accepted for who we are. We long for careful, insightful appreciation of our characters and interests. This was, if things went tolerably well, a little like what happened to us in earliest childhood, when a kindly adult, through the quality of their love, spared us any requirement to impress or, as we might put it, to market ourselves. In those early years, we did not need assiduously to 'sell' who we were; we did not have to smile in exaggerated ways, sound happier than we were, put on seductive accents or compress what we had to say into memorable jingles. We could take our time, hesitate, whisper, be a little elusive and complex and as serious as we needed to be – sure that another would be there to find, decode and accept us. Everything we learnt of love ran counter to the mechanisms of commercialisation.

It is no wonder if we harbour within us a degree of instinctive revulsion against commercial strictures. The need not to sell ourselves aggressively was not just part of an earlier, simpler point in the history of the world (as scholars rightly point out); it was, more poignantly, also a moment in each of our personal histories, to which we may always long to return.

V
Scale

One of the strangest aspects of work is that we don't do it solely, or sometimes even principally, for money. This makes us vulnerable not just to poverty, but also to crises of a more psychological kind. We harbour a demanding ambition to find work that can provide us with something that can best be captured by the word 'meaning'. We hunger for this meaning quite as much as we crave status or enrichment. Meaningful work comprises any activity that impacts positively on another's life, either by reducing suffering or increasing pleasure – a definition that can encompass everything from the life-saving interventions of the cardiac surgeon to the seductive efforts of a pastry chef or Anatolian rug-weaver.

In truth, the vast majority of jobs contribute in some way to the welfare of others. Only a very few are properly devoid of meaning; for example, a career devoted to making fake remedies for hair loss or cancer, or one encouraging those on low incomes to gamble more. However, crucially, a great many jobs are in the odd position of being meaningful while not in any way feeling meaningful.

This problem is rife in the modern age for a very particular reason: the changes in the scale and tempo of work ushered in by industrialisation. Most work now takes place within gigantic organisations that are engaged in a variety of large, complicated and slow-moving projects – and where it can therefore be hard to derive, on a daily basis, any tangible sense of having improved anyone else's life in any way. The customer and the end product are, in the gigantic structures of modernity, simply too far-flung in space and too distant in time. It can be hard to reassure ourselves of our worth and purpose when we are only a single unit among a 20,000-strong team on four continents pushing forward a project that might be ready in five years.

There are sound reasons why the work practices of large organisations proceed at a glacial pace. Product development in sectors such as aeronautics and banking, oil and pharmaceuticals cannot happen overnight. The time frames are logical, but in terms of individual experience, they go directly against our natural, deeply embedded preference for a rapidly unfolding story.

The ancient Greek philosopher Aristotle (385 BC– 323 BC) observed that a key requirement for a satisfying piece of theatre was that it should be over relatively quickly. There might be tensions and complications and unexpected changes of direction, but in a few hours and three acts, there should be a feeling of genuine completion.

It's not just in theatre that speed is attractive. The concentration of action also helps to explain the appeal of sport. In ninety minutes, a football match can take us from a perfect, neutral start to a precise result. However, if football were like modern work in terms of scale and pace, one can imagine it unfolding on eighteen pitches with twenty-two balls and 10,800 players kicking around for thousands of days without any overview of the progress of the game. By the standards of our innate longings, our work unfolds in a disordered, overextended and confusing way.

Our labour feels meaningful not only when it is fast, but also when we get to witness the ways we are helping others; when we can leave the office, factory or shop with an impression of having fixed a problem in someone else's life. This pleasure too is threatened by scale. In the massive organisations of modernity, we may be so distant from the end users of our products and services as to be unable to derive any real benefit from our constructive role in their lives. Spending days improving terms on contracts in the logistics industry truly will lead to a

Our labour feels meaningful not only when it is fast, but also when we get to witness the ways we are helping others.

moment when a couple can contentedly enjoy some ginger biscuits together in front of the TV; optimising data management across different parts of an aerospace firm – along with thousands of other coordinated efforts – truly will contribute to the moment when a young family can bond together on a beach holiday. The connections are genuine, but they may be so extended and convoluted as to feel dispiritingly flimsy and unreal in our minds.

It's a tantalising paradox, and a kind of tragedy, that because of the unavoidable scale of modern work, we may pass our lives helping other people – and yet, day to day, be burdened by a harrowing feeling of having made no difference whatsoever.

VI
Competition

At the heart of how all individuals function, there is a dream of security: security from humiliation, penury, dependence, arbitrary dismissal and uncertainty.

At the heart of how a modern capitalist economy functions, there is a dream of competitive advantage: one based on the intelligent exploitation of invested capital, on the effective deployment of technology, raw material and labour to reduce costs and improve quality and the triumph over competitors so as to maximise shareholder return.

At certain points, these two longings – those of individuals and those of capitalism – seem inherently aligned. At other points, it can seem as if our own well-being has grown entirely irrelevant to the economic machine in which we are enmeshed. We generally don't kick the machine; we are far more inclined to blame ourselves. There is, after all, always enough evidence of people who thrive and succeed to suggest to us that the fault must lie with something we have done. But in our more politically engaged moments, we may dare to complain that the system is not working 'as it should'.

Ironically, at precisely such moments, it is probably

Our mistake
has been to
confuse our own
ambitions
for happiness
with the goals
of the overall
economy.

working very well; it's just that it was never intended to work in the way we would like – for our own well-being. Capitalism does not place the longings and aspirations of the labour force at the heart of its operations (the clue to its essential concerns lies in its name). It was not made to ensure that we have secure, good lives, plenty of time off and pleasant relationships with our families; it was made to maximise shareholder return. Labour has exactly the same status within capitalism as other production inputs, neither more nor less. Alongside rent, the price of fuel, plant, technology and taxes, labour (people) is just another cost. That it happens to be a 'cost' that cries, needs time off, has fragile nerves, sometimes catches the flu and in extremis commits suicide is – at most – a puzzling inconvenience. We should not believe that there is anything faulty about capitalism simply because we have minimal security of employment, little time to see our families, a lot of stress and an uncertain future. These belong to the very conditions that help the system to work well. Our mistake, which has imposed a heavy internal burden on us, has been to confuse our own ambitions for happiness with the goals of the overall economy.

We have innocently viewed a range of anxieties and fears as incidental and solvable, when they are in fact basic necessities for the correct functioning of enterprise. The first and largest of these is the fear of dismissal. A capitalist economy could not work well without it. It is a precondition of efficient business both that existing labour can be removed swiftly and cheaply and that there should be a ready supply of cooperative replacements. Unemployment is not a tragedy for business; it contributes to a willing pool of talent with low bargaining power.

Even the collapse and shuttering of whole firms is not to be lamented overall. Inefficient players who have failed to read market signals have to close, and their capital has to be deployed elsewhere. There is nothing less healthy for capitalism than an economy in which venerable firms, some perhaps very long established and with thousands of loyal workers within them, can't regularly and cleanly go bust.

The relationship we form with a company may last as long as a marriage, and we may give it as much time and devotion as we would give to a partner. But this is a relationship that should, for capitalism to flourish, be close to abusive, because our 'spouse' must at any point be allowed, on the grounds that they could save themselves

3% a year, fire us and take up with a more cooperative and flexible rival in Vietnam or Bolivia.

We have taken care to construct a world where, in many areas, there is an extreme sensitivity to upset and distress. We have rigorous health and safety requirements to ensure that people don't fall off ladders or strain their backs when moving heavy boxes. We make sure that words aren't used to demean or prejudice minorities. Kindergartens present a moving picture of our care for the next generation. Yet in the core area of our work, we operate in a system that is – from an emotional point of view – nothing short of inhuman. But through more sober economic lenses, it isn't anything as alarming: it is merely admirably competitive.

A second fear that prevails is that of not having done enough. We lie awake at night worrying about certain tasks we failed to perform. We cannot stop thinking about what certain competitors may be up to. We panic about the upcoming financial results. We don't sleep very well any more.

This too makes sense. It used to be far tougher on capitalists. Regular breaks used to be mandated. Religion was responsible for many of them; it told people that they should down tools and honour something far more important than their work, like the majesty of the creator of the whole world. This glance upwards to the heavens relativised and calmed the workforce; it put things in perspective and lent a relieving sense that those packages in the warehouse could probably be sent next week after all. On a bad day, there might even be a sermon reminding people to treat workers like God's children and to respect the holiness of every individual, however lowly.

In certain countries, labour organised itself and demanded that everyone in the company had to be given decent conditions and the odd holiday, or else the staff would walk out on strike. There were angry marches and some insane demands to restrict who could be fired and when.

There were some very frustrating limits to technology as well. There was the post, but it took an age. You might have to wait two weeks for a letter and there might be little to do in that time other than check up on the garden, go for long walks, read three Russian novels and talk to the children. Travel for work took an equal eternity. You might be sent to Hamburg by the firm, which could take four whole days, three of them at sea, some of them spent slowly eating kartoffelsalat and schnitzel, chatting to fellow passengers and staring out from the ship's window at the wheat fields near Neuharlingersiel.

It has been a miracle and an unbounded relief for capitalism that this painful age has at last passed. Religion now seldom gets in the way. Its irritating, calming pieties have been replaced by far more robust and motivating narratives drawn from social Darwinism. The labour movement has been effectively pulverised by flattering ambitious workers into believing that they would gain far more by ditching their fellow Indians and aiming to become chiefs themselves. Technology has at last made it possible for the line between leisure and work to be erased. We've been able to give people phones to make sure they are findable at all times and incentivised them to regard these devices as toys for their benefit rather than glorified tracking bracelets for their firms. Travel has been hugely speeded up too, so it is now possible to squeeze in meetings on a couple of continents in just a single day. There is blessedly little time left that a worker can call their own.

The consequence is that we now have almost no energy

left to invest in our personal lives. We constantly search for that elusive holy grail quaintly described by magazines as 'work/life balance'. But anyone who sincerely believes that such an equilibrium might be possible has not begun to understand the logic of capitalism.

Work and love are our two greatest idols. But they are also locked in mortal combat. Work tends to win. The complaints against work from within love are notorious: we are never around, we are always tired, we never give our partner our wholehearted attention, we are obsessive about the office. It is helpful to recognise that modern ideas of love were invented in the late 18th century by artistic people who didn't have real jobs and therefore made great play of the importance of spending time with a lover explaining and sharing feelings and recounting the movements of one's heart. Unfortunately, combining Romanticism and modern capitalism, as we are expected to do, is a near-impossible task. The impressive philosophy of Romantic love – with its emphasis on intimacy and openness – sits very badly alongside the requirements of working routines that fill our heads with complex demands, keep us away from home for long stretches and render us insecure about our positions in a competitive environment.

According to the Romantic ideal, a lover can be kind and good only when they readily communicate their feelings. But the level of openness this assumes is wholly at odds with the realities of work. After a tricky day (or week), our mind's are likely to be numb with worries and duties. We may not feel like doing much besides sitting in silence, staring at the kitchen appliances, running through a series of dramas and crises. Such preoccupation is not pleasant to witness: it risks expressing itself in a range of not very endearing symptoms: grunting, sighing, brooding silence and a short-fused temper. The most innocuous-sounding question about how the day might have gone can elicit a growl – then, if it is repeated, an explosion.

If there is consolation to be found, it lies in knowing enough history to realise that failure isn't personal. It isn't one's own incompetence or lack of drive that has set one's work and private life at loggerheads. We just happen to be living at a point in time when two big, opposed themes are at war, when we have demanding ideas about the needs of families and relationships and equally demanding ideas about work, efficiency, profit and competition. Both are founded on crucial insights; both aim to monopolise our lives. We deserve a high dose of sympathy for the situation we find ourselves in.

VII
Collaboration

One of the most frightening aspects of working life is that we will, unless we are the beneficiaries of extreme good fortune, be required to have colleagues. The colleague is a creature who, endured over any length of time in situations of high stress and procedural complexity, presents one of the greatest threats to calm, composure and soundness of mind.

It is noteworthy that, in the 19th century, one specific working environment developed into a hugely popular subject for painters: the artist's studio. Archetypal paintings of studios showed high-ceilinged rooms with large windows, views over neighbouring rooftops, sparse furniture, messy tables covered in tubes of paint, and half-finished masterpieces propped up against the walls. There was one additional factor that particularly enticed the collective imagination: there was no one in the studio apart from the artist. At exactly the time when more and more people were being gathered into ever-larger offices and experiencing for the first time all the attendant compromises and constrictions, there grew a craving for paintings of an alternative utopia; a place of work consolingly free of the damnable presence of the colleague.

We have ended up in offices not by bad luck, but by the unavoidable fact that the mighty tasks of modern capitalism simply cannot be undertaken on one's own. It remains (sadly) impossible to run an airline or to manage a bank solo.

The problem with colleagues begins with the fundamental challenge associated with trying to communicate the contents of one's mind to another person. When we are doing things by ourselves, the flow of information is immediate and friction-free. If we could listen in to our inner monologues, they would be made up of a speedy and baffling series of assertions and jumbled words: 'narr, yes. Come on! Do it till then, after no more. Ah, nearly, no, no, no, no, back . . . OK, got it, got it . . . No! Yes. That's fine. So.'

But when we collaborate, we must laboriously turn the stream of consciousness that only we can follow into unwieldy, externally comprehensible messages. We have to translate feelings into language, temper our wilder impulses and affix paragraphs to intuitions in order to generate prompts and suggestions that have a chance of being effective in the minds of other people.

By a painful quirk of psychology, others can't by instinct alone understand what we need and want – although it can seem as though they surely must. The realisation that other people are not like us and can't guess what we want takes a long time to sink in – and the idea perhaps always remains a bit foreign and unjust. In their earliest days, babies simply don't realise that their mothers are separate beings, and so get frustrated when these reluctant appendages don't by magic obey their unstated wishes. Only after a long and difficult process of development (if ever) can a child realise that their parent is truly a distinct individual, and that, in order to make themselves understood by them, they will have to do more than grunt and imagine solutions in their heads. It can be the work of a lifetime, in which the office occupies a particularly painful passage, to gradually accept the impossibility of mutual mind reading.

If this were not bad enough, many colleagues are at risk of not sharing our underlying vision of what should be done. They have contrary opinions, their own quirks, pet peeves and obsessive interests. To get our point across and assuage their resistance requires us to deploy a battery of diplomatic skills. At the very moment when, agitated and overwhelmed, we would like simply to shout or bark, we have no option but to charm. This is because the colleague is, on top of it all, extremely sensitive. Unless they are spoken to correctly, they will become offended, develop grudges, start to cry or report us to a superior.

The imperative to be pleasant at work is a novel one that we are still getting used to. In the olden days, brusqueness used to be the norm: it was a good way to get people to turn a boat swiftly starboard, push coal trolleys faster, or increase the rate of production at the blast furnace in a steel mill. When most work was physical, management could be abrupt; workers could feel underappreciated or bullied and nevertheless perform their required tasks to perfection. Emotional distress didn't hold things up. You could still operate the brick-making machine at maximum speed, even if you hated the manager, or clean out the stables thoroughly even if you felt the foreman hadn't enquired deeply enough into the nature of your weekend.

But nowadays, most jobs require a high degree of psychological well-being in order to be performed adequately. A wounding comment can destroy a person's productivity for a whole day. Without ample respect, recognition and encouragement, huge sums of money will be wasted in silently resentful moods. If we have any concern for the bottom line, we have no alternative but to try to be a little bit nice.

At the same time, the inability to speak frankly has its own enormous cost. A huge amount of valuable information that should make its way around a company is held back by the imperative not to cause offence. We hold our tongues because we are scared to upset juniors, to alienate colleagues and to ruin our relationships with superiors – and, in the process, insights that might help an organisation to thrive stay locked in individual hearts.

Work relationships are no less tricky than romantic ones, but at least in the latter we have a basic sense of security that enables us to speak our minds and make the necessary cathartic moves – to call the other person a fuckwit and compress a range of ideas into the occasional expletive-loaded outburst. The office environment misses out on the cleansing frankness seemingly possible only when two people know they will have the option of having sex together after a bust-up.

At the heart of our office agonies is the complaint that we seldom like our colleagues as people. In a better world, we would be unlikely ever to want to spend any time with such disturbing, and often unlikely, figures. We shouldn't be surprised by our daily discomfort, given that these people were never picked out on the basis of psychological compatibility. We were formed into a unit because they had a range of technical and commercial competences necessary for a task, not because they were fun lunch companions or were graced with a pleasing manner. We are like the unfortunate bride in a power-marriage in the Middle Ages. A princess would be obliged to marry a certain prince because he owned an important lead mine or because the archers in his country were especially proficient. It would have been nice if the two liked each other as well, but the stakes were generally too high for this to be a relevant factor. The success of the realm depended on such matters as access to raw materials and military strength, not on whether one partner had a maddening giggle or a daunting overbite.

There is yet another challenge posed by colleagues. Corporations and businesses are fundamentally hierarchical, with an ever-smaller number of desirable, better-rewarded places at the pinnacle. A naive outsider might imagine that career progression would be determined by clear, precise and public determinants of merit, probably of a technical or financial sort, akin to the straightforward nature of the examination results we all grew up with. But the reality is that, in many occupations, no verifiable measure of performance is available. Factors of success are numerous, opaque and shifting. What decides who is promoted is not talent per se, but success at a range of dark psychological arts best summed up by the term 'politics'.

Political skill has woefully little in common with the reasons we were trained and hired to do our jobs in the first place. We may, as part of a good business education, have spent years studying how to navigate a balance sheet, analyse competitors, negotiate contracts, and administer a logistics chain. But when we reach the office, we will be confronted by other, less familiar, kinds of challenges: the person at the desk opposite us with the charming manner who enthusiastically agrees with whomever they're speaking to, yet harbours a range of toxic reservations and privately pursues their own undeclared agenda; the person who responds to polite criticism or well-meaning feedback with hurt and fury; the person who pretends to be our friend, but takes the credit for our best efforts.

In such situations, the most unlovely qualities may turn out to be the most necessary ones: the capacity to quietly accept glory for things that were not truly our doing; to distance ourselves from errors in which we were heavily implicated; to subtly foreground the failings of otherwise quite able colleagues; to turn cold at key moments towards emotionally vulnerable superiors; to flatter while not appearing to do so; to mould our views to suit the currently ascendant attitudes.

Such grey, underhand strategies are not easy to pick up, and they may feel impossible for us to practise if we pride ourselves on being straightforward, direct or even just somewhat ethical. Yet we can be certain that every high-minded refusal of duplicity will carry a heavy, perhaps career-damaging, cost.

Our problems with the collegial nature of work are compounded by the implication that matters should be straightforward. Our inevitable difficulties are aggravated by notions that offices are at heart giant families; that colleagues can be friends; that honesty is rewarded, and that talent will win out. Kindly sentimentality is, in the end, just a disguised version of cruelty. It might be simpler if, in dark moments, we could simply admit to what we know in our hearts: that it would obviously be better if we could be shot of the whole business of colleagues and spend our days, as we used to so well, sitting comfortably on the floor in our room assembling cargo planes, city car parks and bear picnics on our own.

VIII
Equal
Opportunity

The modern world was founded upon, and continues to be enthused by, the promise of equal opportunity – and infinite possibility – for all. Each of us grows up with a sense that a great deal could be possible. Adults listen respectfully when small children suggest they might travel to the Space Station, run the country or play for a winning team. Such feats aren't wholly fanciful, particularly when considered through parental eyes. Similarly transformative journeys are everywhere to behold. It would be churlish to ignore that extraordinary destinies are a regular feature of modern life.

The idea of equal opportunity springs from the most generous side of our nature and has been responsible for inspiring the most indispensable achievements. But it has also, unwittingly and far more quietly, been the source of unending sorrow. American psychologist William James (1842–1910) recognised the anxiety created by societies that promise their inhabitants infinite opportunities for social transformation and career success – and then can't always deliver. For James, satisfaction with ourselves does not require us to succeed in every area. We are not always humiliated by failing at things; we are humiliated only if we first invested our pride and sense of worth in a given achievement and then did not reach it. Our ambitions determine what we will interpret as a triumph and what must count as a failure. 'With no attempt there can be no failure; with no failure no humiliation. So our self-esteem in this world depends entirely on what we back ourselves to be and do,' wrote James. 'It is determined by the ratio of our actualities to our supposed potentialities'. Thus:

$$\text{Self-esteem} = \frac{\text{Success}}{\text{Pretensions}}$$

The problem with the modern world is that it does not stop lending us extremely high expectations and inviting us to dream, and then leaving us with a bitter sense of failure.

A firm belief in the limitations of life was once one of humankind's most important assets; a bulwark against bitterness and envy; a wisdom cruelly undermined by the ideology of infinite expectation proclaimed by the modern worldview. Feeling 'successful' might not be so much about having many things, as a matter of having what we long for. Success is not an absolute. It is relative to desire; every time we seek something we cannot afford, we grow poorer, whatever our resources.

Insofar as advanced societies provide us with many options for success, they appear to be helping us. But in truth, the net effect may be to humiliate us: through a language of unlimited opportunity, these societies keep open a permanent gap between who we want to be and what we have achieved. There are two ways to make people feel more successful: to give them more success, or to narrow their ambitions. Modern capitalism has in certain areas succeeded spectacularly at the first option, but, by stretching our aspirations, it has left a painful gap between our hopes and our reality – a gap we are left to fill with shame and rage.

IX
Meritocracy

Modern politicians across the political spectrum show remarkable agreement on one goal: that of creating a fully meritocratic society, a society in which all those who make it to the top do so because of their own talents and abilities, rather than due to unfair privilege, upper-class parents or connections. The stated aim is to create a hierarchy based on ability, replacing chinless halfwits with the meritorious, wherever they may be found and whatever age, colour or gender they might be.

This meritocratic ideal has brought opportunity to millions. Gifted and intelligent individuals who for centuries were held down within immobile, caste-like hierarchies are now free to express their talents on a more or less level playing field. We have largely turned the page on a world that was filled with rulers who were too sick or stupid to govern; lords who couldn't manage their estates; commanders who didn't understand the principles of battle; peasants who were brighter than their masters, and maids who knew more than their mistresses. No longer is background an impassable obstacle to advancement. An element of justice has finally entered the distribution of rewards.

But there is a darker side to the idea of meritocracy: if

we truly believe that we have created (or could one day create) a world where the successful truly merited all their success, it follows that we have to hold the 'failures' exclusively responsible for their failures. In a meritocratic age, an element of justice enters into the distribution of wealth, but also of poverty. Low status comes to seem not merely regrettable, but also deserved.

Succeeding financially (without inheritance or contacts) in an economic meritocracy endows individuals with an element of personal validation that the nobleman of old, who had been given his money and his castle by his father, had never been able to feel. But, at the same time, financial failure has become associated with a sense of shame that the peasant of old, denied all chances in life, had also been spared. The question of why, if one is good, clever or able, one is still poor becomes infinitely more acute and painful for the unsuccessful to have to answer (to themselves and others) in a new meritocratic age.

There has turned out to be no shortage of people willing to answer the question on behalf of the 'failed'. For a certain constituency, it is clear that the failures owe their position to their own stupidity and degeneracy. With the rise of an economic meritocracy, in certain quarters, the failures have moved from being described as 'unfortunates', the target of the charity and guilt of the paternally-minded rich, to being described as 'losers', fair targets of contempt in the eyes of robust self-made individuals, who are disinclined to feel ashamed about their mansions or shed crocodile tears for those whose company they have escaped. In the harsher climate of opinion that can gestate in meritocratic societies, it has become possible to argue that social hierarchy rigorously reflects the qualities of the members on every rung of the ladder so that conditions are already in place for the good people to succeed and the dummies to flounder – attenuating the need for charity, welfare, redistributive measures or simple compassion. To the injury of poverty, a meritocratic system has added the insult of humiliation.

It is a symptom of our faith in meritocracy that it has largely become impossible to explain away professional failure as the result of 'bad luck'. Although it is granted that luck maintains a theoretical role in shaping our careers, the evaluation of people proceeds, in practical terms, as if they could fairly be held responsible for their biographies. It would seem unduly (and even suspiciously) modest to ascribe a victory to 'good luck' and, more importantly in this context, pitiable to blame defeat on the opposite. Winners make their own luck, insists the modern mantra, which would have puzzled the ancient Roman worshippers of the Goddess of Fortune.

We are paying a heavy price for our faith in a fairer world: that of having to take full responsibility for what we achieve and, more poignantly, fail to achieve, in the course of our lives.

We are paying a heavy price for our faith in a fairer world.

X
Conclusion

We need an extraordinary run of good fortune to make a success of our careers: an early understanding of our talents and interests; the right educational opportunities; the best kind of inferiority complex; a benign political environment; physical and mental health; confidence, stamina, friends; a lack of scandals; a propitious number of lucky breaks; clumsy enemies; supportive relationships; an untragic sexuality; an upbeat temperament... And all this needs to be in place not for one or two years, but – so that we'll be more than mere flashes-in-the-pan – for four decades at least.

We should not be surprised if we don't quite get there. We were not uncommonly stupid. We were tricked into misunderstanding the statistics of success, in mistaking the unique for the possible. We longed for glorious destinies, of which there are always far fewer than there are numbers of the aspiring and the ardent. The game is close to rigged so as to cause heartbreak on a mass scale, although the sadness rarely recognises itself as collective, and is experienced in each individual soul as a uniquely personal defeat.

Our minds are partly to blame. We are hardwired for ambitious plans. It isn't our nature to rest with what is already to hand or easy to reach. We are inherently ungrateful, and feel alive only when we have taken on a struggle that has a good chance of crushing us. Even those we think of as successes will secretly nurse dreams they have had to forego. There is always a gap between achievement and desire. Feeling like a failure is the inevitable price for harbouring any sort of ambition.

We would be mad not to strive for success, but we will end up demented if we don't also, over time, develop capacities for making peace with defeat. The task begins with forewarning, with a secure, calm, dark knowledge that we will inevitably be tripped up along the way.

We need to be free of a sense of persecution in this regard. It truly was not personal. Our dreams are like a fragile house of twigs exposed to a hurricane. We should stop fixating on what life has done to us, and check in with what it is doing to others every day – the ones who never make it into the magazines; the legions of the quietly despairing and dying. It is no loser's counsel to work with a vivid sense of how much worse it might, and will still, get.

We should make ourselves at home with mediocrity.

Feeling
like a failure
is the inevitable
price for
harbouring
any sort of
ambition.

'Failure' sounds like too extreme a word for something that is so normal. We should be more alive to its ubiquity and wear it with greater ease, as something – like death – that is coming for us all. We might laugh defiantly at its embrace, refuse to be cowed by it and mock our pretensions without remorse or self-importance.

It isn't easy, of course, that we are typically surrounded by people trapped in a toxic ideology of ambition. The first question we will be asked when meeting almost any new person is: 'What do you do?' If our answer is insufficiently elevated, we will at once notice the loss of interest and our total dispensability to most members of the race.

These things continue to matter more than they should. We should try to be gentle on ourselves. We could reduce how often we'll be exposed to this sort of judgement. We might attempt to develop an identity not so exclusively connected to achievement, so that who we are becomes bound up not just with salary and rank, but also our character, our relationships, our interests and our unmonetised and unpublished skills.

We should learn the wisdom of a degree of melancholy in relation to our work, founded on an understanding that the sorrow isn't just about us; that our suffering belongs to humanity in general. This should not make us desperate, but rather more forgiving of our failure, kinder to that of others and better able to focus on what really matters, while there is still time.

Picture Credits

p.31
Gargoyle Sailsbury Cathredral, Wiltshire
Coombs Images / Alamy Stock Photo

p.32
Sussex chair, c. 1860
Webb, Philip Speakman (designer)
Morris & Co. (maker)
© Victoria and Albert Museum, London

p.35
Aluminium Chair EA 103
Charles & Ray Eames
Photo: Marc Eggimann © Vitra

The School of Life is dedicated to developing emotional intelligence – believing that a range of our most persistent problems are created by a lack of self-understanding, compassion and communication. We operate from ten physical campuses around the world, including London, Amsterdam, Seoul and Melbourne. We produce films, run classes, offer therapy and make a range of psychological products. **The School of Life Press** publishes books on the most important issues of emotional life. Our titles are designed to entertain, educate, console and transform.

THESCHOOLOFLIFE.COM